D1558805

Connect with us
IG: @LeapsofJoy
www.pocketfulofjoy.com

Giving you a boost of positivity, truth, and encouragement

My Name is

[   ]

and I Choose
Joy!

JOY!

IN YOUR PRESENCE IS JOYFUL ABUNDANCE, AT YOUR
RIGHT HAND THERE ARE PLEASURES FOREVER.
PSALM 16:11B ISV

JOY!

RESTORE TO ME THE JOY OF YOUR SALVATION, AND
MAKE ME WILLING TO OBEY YOU.
PSALM 51:12 NLT

_____

_____

_____

_____

_____

_____

_____

_____

_____

_____

_____

_____

_____

_____

_____

_____

_____

_____

_____

_____

I'M CONVINCED THAT NOTHING CAN SEPARATE US
FROM GOD'S LOVE IN CHRIST JESUS OUR LORD: NOT
DEATH OR LIFE, NOT ANGELS OR RULERS, NOT PRESENT
THINGS OR FUTURE THINGS, NOT POWERS
ROMANS 8:38 CEB

JOY!

WHEN ANXIETY WAS GREAT WITHIN ME, YOUR
CONSOLATION BROUGHT ME JOY.
PSALM 94:19 NIV

SO THAT I MAY COME TO YOU WITH JOY, BY GOD'S
WILL, AND IN YOUR COMPANY BE REFRESHED.
ROMANS 15:32 NIV

JOY!

FOR THE LORD TAKES DELIGHT IN HIS PEOPLE;HE
CROWNS THE HUMBLE WITH VICTORY.
PSALM 149:4 NIV

JOY!

YOUR STATUTES ARE MY HERITAGE FOREVER;THEY ARE
THE JOY OF MY HEART.
PSALM 119:11 NIV

JOY!

NO, DESPITE ALL THESE THINGS, OVERWHELMING
VICTORY IS OURS THROUGH CHRIST, WHO LOVED US.
ROMANS 8:37 NLT

MY HEART AND SOUL EXPLODE WITH JOY—FULL OF GLORY! EVEN MY BODY WILL REST CONFIDENT AND SECURE.
PSALM 16:9 TPT

JOY!

LET ME HEAR THE SOUNDS OF JOY AND GLADNESS; AND
THOUGH YOU HAVE CRUSHED ME AND BROKEN ME, I
WILL BE HAPPY ONCE AGAIN.
PSALM 51:9 GNT

JOY!

LET US COME BEFORE HIM WITH THANKSGIVING AND
SING JOYFUL SONGS OF PRAISE.
PSALM 95:2 GNT

I FIND JOY IN THE WAY [SHOWN BY] YOUR WRITTEN
INSTRUCTIONS MORE THAN I FIND JOY IN ALL KINDS OF
RICHES.
PSALM 119:14A GWT

I HAVE TOLD YOU THIS SO THAT MY JOY MAY BE IN YOU
AND THAT YOUR JOY MAY BE COMPLETE.
JOHN 15:11 NIV

JOY!

I WILL BE FILLED WITH JOY BECAUSE OF YOU. I WILL
SING PRAISES TO YOUR NAME, O MOST HIGH.
PSALM 9:2 NLT

EVEN THOUGH YOU DON'T SEE HIM NOW, YOU TRUST HIM
AND SO REJOICE WITH A GLORIOUS JOY THAT IS TOO
MUCH FOR WORDS.
1 PETER 1:8B CEB

JOY!

MANY SORROWS COME TO THE WICKED, BUT UNFAILING
LOVE SURROUNDS THOSE WHO TRUST THE LORD
PSALM 32:10 NLT

JOY!

TRUST IN THE LORD FOREVER, FOR THE LORD,
THE LORD HIMSELF, IS THE ROCK ETERNAL.
ISAIAH 26:4 NIV

JOY!

BUT I TRUST YOUR MERCY. MY HEART FINDS JOY IN YOUR
SALVATION.
PSALM 13:5 GW

JOY!

BUT THE ANGEL SAID TO THEM, "DO NOT BE AFRAID. I
BRING YOU GOOD NEWS THAT WILL CAUSE GREAT JOY
FOR ALL THE PEOPLE."
LUKE 2:10 NIV

CLAP YOUR HANDS, ALL YOU PEOPLES! SHOUT TO GOD
WITH A LOUD CRY OF JOY!
PSALM 47:1 ISV

YOU HAVE ENLARGED THE NATION AND INCREASED THEIR
JOY; THEY REJOICE BEFORE YOU AS PEOPLE REJOICE AT
THE HARVEST
ISAIAH 9:3 NIV

SHOUT ALOUD AND SING FOR JOY, PEOPLE OF ZION,
FOR GREAT IS THE HOLY ONE OF ISRAEL AMONG YOU.
ISAIAH 12:6 NIV

BUT I AM LIKE AN OLIVE TREE, THRIVING IN THE HOUSE
OF GOD. I WILL ALWAYS TRUST IN GOD'S UNFAILING
LOVE.
PSALM 52:8 NLT

JOY!

DON'T BE PULLED IN DIFFERENT DIRECTIONS OR
WORRIED ABOUT A THING. BE SATURATED IN
PRAYER...OFFERING YOUR FAITH-FILLED REQUESTS
BEFORE GOD WITH OVERFLOWING GRATITUDE...
PHILIPPIANS 4:6 TPT

_____

_____

_____

_____

_____

_____

_____

_____

_____

_____

_____

_____

_____

_____

_____

_____

_____

_____

_____

_____

_____

_____

_____

AS WE TRUST, WE REJOICE WITH AN UNCONTAINED JOY
FLOWING FROM YAHWEH!
PSALM 33:21 TPT

JOY!

THE LORD PROTECTS AND DEFENDS ME; I TRUST IN HIM.
HE GIVES ME HELP AND MAKES ME GLAD; I PRAISE HIM
WITH JOYFUL SONGS.
PSALM 28:7 GNT

JOY!

I WILL INSTRUCT YOU AND TEACH YOU IN THE WAY YOU
SHOULD GO; I WILL COUNSEL YOU WITH MY LOVING
EYE ON YOU.
PSALM 32:8 NIV

JOY!

SO GOD BROUGHT OUT HIS CHOSEN ONES WITH
SINGING; WITH A JOYFUL SHOUT THEY WERE SET FREE!
PSALM 105:43 TPT

JOY!

AND FASTEN YOUR THOUGHTS ON EVERY GLORIOUS
WORK OF GOD, PRAISING HIM ALWAYS.
PHILIPPIANS 4:8B TPT

JOY!

CONSIDER IT PURE JOY, MY BROTHERS AND SISTERS,
WHENEVER YOU FACE TRIALS OF MANY KINDS,
JAMES 1:2 NIV

_____

_____

_____

_____

_____

_____

_____

_____

_____

_____

_____

_____

_____

_____

_____

_____

_____

_____

_____

_____

_____

MY SOUL WILL FIND JOY IN THE LORD AND BE JOYFUL
ABOUT HIS SALVATION.
PSALM 35:9 GW

HONOR AND MAJESTY SURROUND HIM; STRENGTH AND
JOY FILL HIS DWELLING.
1 CHRONICLES 16:27 NLT

_____

_____

_____

_____

_____

_____

_____

_____

_____

_____

_____

_____

_____

_____

_____

_____

_____

_____

_____

_____

_____

_____

_____

BUT LET ALL WHO TAKE REFUGE IN YOU REJOICE; LET
THEM SING JOYFUL PRAISES FOREVER.
PSALM 5:11A NLT

THEY TOLD THEM—MUCH TO EVERYONE'S JOY—THAT THE
GENTILES, TOO, WERE BEING CONVERTED.
ACTS 15:3A NLT

SO REJOICE IN THE LORD AND BE GLAD, ALL YOU WHO
OBEY HIM! SHOUT FOR JOY, ALL YOU WHOSE HEARTS
ARE PURE!
PSALM 32:11 NLT

JOY!

THEY WILL ENTER ZION WITH SINGING; EVERLASTING
JOY WILL CROWN THEIR HEADS. GLADNESS AND JOY
WILL OVERTAKE THEM, AND SORROW...WILL FLEE AWAY.
ISAIAH 35:10 NIV

JOY!

TASTE AND SEE THAT THE LORD IS GOOD. OH, THE JOYS
OF THOSE WHO TAKE REFUGE IN HIM!
PSALM 34:8 NLT

LET THE TREES OF THE FOREST SING FOR JOY BEFORE
THE LORD...GIVE THANKS TO THE LORD, FOR HE IS
GOOD!
1 CHRONICLES 16:33-34 NLT

JOY!

I HAVE TOLD YOU THESE THINGS, SO THAT IN ME YOU
MAY HAVE PEACE.
JOHN 16:33 NIV

JOY!

THE LORD GIVES STRENGTH TO HIS PEOPLE;
THE LORD BLESSES HIS PEOPLE WITH PEACE.
PSALM 29:11 NIV

PRAISE GOD WITH SHOUTS OF JOY, ALL PEOPLE!
PSALM 66:1 GNT

JOY!

FOR THE KINGDOM OF GOD IS NOT A MATTER OF
EATING AND DRINKING, BUT OF RIGHTEOUSNESS, PEACE
AND JOY IN THE HOLY SPIRIT.
ROMANS 14:17 NIV

IN HIM OUR HEARTS FIND JOY. IN HIS HOLY NAME WE
TRUST.
PSALM 33:21 GW

JOY!

WITH JOY YOU WILL DRINK DEEPLY FROM THE FOUNTAIN
OF SALVATION... TELL THE NATIONS WHAT HE HAS
DONE...
ISAIAH 12:3-4 NLT

EVEN THE WILDERNESS AND DESERT WILL BE GLAD IN
THOSE DAYS. THE WASTELAND WILL REJOICE ....
ISAIAH 35:1 NIV

JOY!

SHOUT WITH JOY TO THE LORD, ALL THE EARTH!
PSALM 100:1 NLT

THE LORD SAID, "SING FOR JOY, PEOPLE OF
JERUSALEM! I AM COMING TO LIVE AMONG YOU!"
ZECHARIAH 2:10 GNT

RIGHTEOUS PEOPLE WILL FIND JOY IN THE LORD AND
TAKE REFUGE IN HIM.
PSALM 64:10A GW

SING AND SHOUT FOR JOY, PEOPLE OF ISRAEL! REJOICE
WITH ALL YOUR HEART, JERUSALEM!
ZEPHANIAH 3:14 GNT

JOY!

REJOICE GREATLY, DAUGHTER ZION! ...SEE, YOUR KING
COMES TO YOU, RIGHTEOUS AND HAVING SALVATION,
ZECHARIAH 9:9A NIV

JOY!

GOD OUR SAVIOR SHOWED US HOW GOOD AND KIND
HE IS.
TITUS 3:4 CEV

JOY!

YOUR KINDNESS WILL REWARD YOU, BUT YOUR CRUELTY
WILL DESTROY YOU.
PROVERBS 11:17 NLT

BE KIND AND COMPASSIONATE TO ONE ANOTHER,
FORGIVING EACH OTHER, JUST AS IN CHRIST GOD
FORGAVE YOU.
EPHESIANS 4:32 NIV

JOY!

YOU ARE THE PEOPLE OF GOD; HE LOVED YOU AND
CHOSE YOU FOR HIS OWN. SO THEN, YOU MUST
CLOTHE YOURSELVES WITH COMPASSION, KINDNESS,
HUMILITY, GENTLENESS, AND PATIENCE.
COLOSSIANS 3:12 GNT

YOUR BLESSINGS ARE WITH HIM FOREVER, AND YOUR
PRESENCE FILLS HIM WITH JOY.
PSALM 21:6 GNT

JOY!

BUT REJOICE INASMUCH AS YOU PARTICIPATE IN THE
SUFFERINGS OF CHRIST, SO THAT YOU MAY BE
OVERJOYED WHEN HIS GLORY IS REVEALED.
1 PETER 4:13 NIV

JOY!

BE KIND AND HONEST AND YOU WILL LIVE A LONG LIFE;
OTHERS WILL RESPECT YOU AND TREAT YOU FAIRLY.
PROVERBS 21:21 GNT

JOY!

THEY WILL COME AND SHOUT FOR JOY ON THE HEIGHTS
OF ZION; THEY WILL REJOICE IN THE BOUNTY OF THE
LORD...
JEREMIAH 31:12A NIV

EVEN THE WILDERNESS AND DESERT WILL BE GLAD IN
THOSE DAYS. THE WASTELAND WILL REJOICE ....
ISAIAH 35:1 NIV

JOY!

I WILL TURN THEIR MOURNING INTO JOY. I WILL
...EXCHANGE THEIR SORROW FOR REJOICING.
JEREMIAH 31:13B NLT

JOY!

REJOICE AND BE GLAD, BECAUSE GREAT IS YOUR
REWARD IN HEAVEN.
MATTHEW 5:12A NIV

JOY!

...I CAN CONTINUE TO HELP ALL OF YOU GROW AND
EXPERIENCE THE JOY OF YOUR FAITH.
PHILLIPIANS 1:25B NLT

AT HIS SACRED TENT I WILL SACRIFICE WITH SHOUTS OF
JOY; I WILL SING AND MAKE MUSIC TO THE LORD.
PSALM 27:6 NIV

JOY!

THEY WILL RAVE IN CELEBRATION OF YOUR ABUNDANT
GOODNESS;THEY WILL SHOUT JOYFULLY ABOUT YOUR
RIGHTEOUSNESS
PSALM 145:7 CEB

GIVE THANKS TO THE LORD, FOR HE IS GOOD! HIS
FAITHFUL LOVE ENDURES FOREVER.
PSALM 107:1 NLT

JOY!

... AND YOU WILL REJOICE IN ALL YOU HAVE
ACCOMPLISHED BECAUSE THE LORD YOUR GOD HAS
BLESSED YOU.
DEUTERONOMY 12:7B NLT

LET THEM BRING SONGS OF THANKSGIVING AS THEIR
SACRIFICE. LET THEM TELL IN JOYFUL SONGS WHAT HE
HAS DONE.
PSALM 107:22 GW

JOY!

SONGS OF JOY AND VICTORY ARE SUNG IN THE CAMP
OF THE GODLY. THE STRONG RIGHT ARM OF THE LORD
HAS DONE GLORIOUS THINGS!
PSALM 118:15 NLT

JOY!

EVERYONE HAS HEARD ABOUT YOUR OBEDIENCE, SO I
REJOICE BECAUSE OF YOU;
ROMANS 16:19A NIV

JOY!

THE PEOPLE OF EPHRAIM WILL BECOME LIKE MIGHTY
SOLDIERS... THEIR HEARTS WILL FIND JOY IN THE LORD
ZECHARIAH 10:7 ISV

SING AND SHOUT FOR JOY, PEOPLE OF ISRAEL! REJOICE
WITH ALL YOUR HEART, JERUSALEM!
ZEPHANIAH 3:14 GNT

JOY!

MAY YOUR PRIESTS BE CLOTHED IN GODLINESS; MAY
YOUR LOYAL SERVANTS SING FOR JOY.
PSALM 132:9 NLT

SHOUT FOR JOY TO THE LORD, ALL THE EARTH, BURST
INTO JUBILANT SONG WITH MUSIC
PSALM 98:4 NIV

HE SETS THE TIME FOR SORROW AND THE TIME FOR
JOY, THE TIME FOR MOURNING AND THE TIME FOR
DANCING,
ECCLESIASTES 3:4 GNT

_____

_____

_____

_____

_____

_____

_____

_____

_____

_____

_____

_____

_____

_____

_____

_____

_____

_____

_____

_____

ON THE SEVENTH DAY GOD HAD FINISHED HIS WORK OF
CREATION, SO HE RESTED FROM ALL HIS WORK.
GENESIS 2:2 NLT

JOY!

BUT MAY THE RIGHTEOUS BE GLAD AND REJOICE
BEFORE GOD; MAY THEY BE HAPPY AND JOYFUL.
PSALM 68:3 NIV

HE WILL ONCE AGAIN FILL YOUR MOUTH WITH LAUGHTER
AND YOUR LIPS WITH SHOUTS OF JOY.
JOB 8:21 NLT

_____

_____

_____

_____

_____

_____

_____

_____

_____

_____

_____

_____

_____

_____

_____

_____

_____

_____

_____

_____

_____

_____

FIND JOY IN THE LORD, YOU RIGHTEOUS PEOPLE. GIVE
THANKS TO HIM AS YOU REMEMBER HOW HOLY HE IS.
PSALM 97:12 GW

_..._BE JOYFUL. GROW TO MATURITY. ENCOURAGE EACH
OTHER. LIVE IN HARMONY AND PEACE_...._
2 CORINTHIANS 13:11 NLT

...I REJOICE, AND I SHARE MY JOY WITH ALL OF YOU.
PHILIPPIANS 2:17 ISV

WE ALSO PRAY THAT YOU WILL BE STRENGTHENED WITH
ALL HIS GLORIOUS POWER...MAY YOU BE FILLED WITH JOY
COLOSSIANS 1:11 NLT

_____

_____

_____

_____

_____

_____

_____

_____

_____

_____

_____

_____

_____

_____

_____

_____

_____

_____

_____

_____

BE JOYFUL IN HOPE, PATIENT IN AFFLICTION, FAITHFUL
IN PRAYER.
ROMANS 12:12 NIV

JOY!

HOW CAN WE THANK GOD ENOUGH FOR YOU IN RETURN
FOR ALL THE JOY WE HAVE IN THE PRESENCE OF OUR
GOD BECAUSE OF YOU?
1 THESSALONIANS 3:9 NIV

JOY!

YOUR LOVE HAS GIVEN ME GREAT JOY AND
ENCOURAGEMENT, BECAUSE YOU, BROTHER, HAVE
REFRESHED THE HEARTS OF THE LORD'S PEOPLE.
PHILEMON 1:7 NIV

THIS IS OUR GOD! WE'VE WAITED FOR HIM, AND HE
SAVED US! ...WE WILL KEEP SHOUTING WITH JOY AS WE
FIND OUR BLISS IN HIS SALVATION...
ISAIAH 25:9 TPT

JOY!

YOU HAVE GIVEN THEM GREAT JOY, LORD; YOU HAVE
MADE THEM HAPPY. THEY REJOICE..AS PEOPLE
REJOICE WHEN THEY HARVEST GRAIN....
ISAIAH 9:3 GNT

JOY!

YES, YOU SHOULD REJOICE, AND I WILL SHARE YOUR
JOY.
PHILIPPIANS 2:18 NLT

ALWAYS BE FULL OF JOY IN THE LORD. I SAY IT AGAIN—
REJOICE!
PHILIPPIANS 4:4 NLT

...REJOICE IN THE LORD YOUR GOD! FOR THE RAIN HE
SENDS DEMONSTRATES HIS FAITHFULNESS.
JOEL 2:23 NLT

JOY!

WE ASK HIM TO STRENGTHEN YOU BY HIS GLORIOUS
MIGHT WITH ALL THE POWER YOU NEED TO PATIENTLY
ENDURE EVERYTHING WITH JOY.
COLOSSIANS 1:11 GW

JOY!

MAY ALL WHO ARE GODLY REJOICE IN THE LORD AND
PRAISE HIS HOLY NAME!
PSALM 97:12 NLT

JOY!

GLORY IN HIS HOLY NAME; LET THE HEARTS OF THOSE
WHO SEEK THE LORD REJOICE.
PSALM 105:3 NIV

YET I WILL REJOICE IN THE LORD, I WILL BE JOYFUL IN
GOD MY SAVIOR.
HABAKKUK 3:18 NIV

JOY!

ALWAYS BE JOYFUL.
1 THESSALONIANS 5:16S 5:16 NLT

... I AM GREATLY ENCOURAGED; IN ALL OUR TROUBLES
MY JOY KNOWS NO BOUNDS.
2 CORINTHIANS 7:4 NIV

JOY!

THIS IS THE DAY THE LORD HAS MADE. WE WILL REJOICE
AND BE GLAD IN IT.
PSALM 118:24 NLT

IN MERCY YOU HAVE SEEN MY TROUBLES AND YOU
HAVE CARED FOR ME; EVEN DURING THIS CRISIS IN MY
SOUL I WILL BE RADIANT WITH JOY, FILLED WITH PRAISE
FOR YOUR LOVE AND MERCY
PSALM 31:7 TPT

JOY!

FIXING OUR ATTENTION ON JESUS, THE PIONEER AND
PERFECTER OF THE FAITH, WHO, IN VIEW OF THE JOY
SET BEFORE HIM, ENDURED THE CROSS...AND HAS SAT
DOWN AT THE RIGHT HAND OF THE THRONE OF GOD.
HEBREWS 12:2 ISV

JOY!

IN YOUR PRESENCE IS JOYFUL ABUNDANCE, AT YOUR
RIGHT HAND THERE ARE PLEASURES FOREVER.
PSALM 16:11B ISV

JOY!

RESTORE TO ME THE JOY OF YOUR SALVATION, AND
MAKE ME WILLING TO OBEY YOU.
PSALM 51:12 NLT

_____

_____

_____

_____

_____

_____

_____

_____

_____

_____

_____

_____

_____

_____

_____

_____

_____

_____

_____

_____

_____

_____

_____

I'M CONVINCED THAT NOTHING CAN SEPARATE US
FROM GOD'S LOVE IN CHRIST JESUS OUR LORD: NOT
DEATH OR LIFE, NOT ANGELS OR RULERS, NOT PRESENT
THINGS OR FUTURE THINGS, NOT POWERS
ROMANS 8:38 CEB

JOY!

WHEN ANXIETY WAS GREAT WITHIN ME, YOUR
CONSOLATION BROUGHT ME JOY.
PSALM 94:19 NIV

SO THAT I MAY COME TO YOU WITH JOY, BY GOD'S
WILL, AND IN YOUR COMPANY BE REFRESHED.
ROMANS 15:32 NIV

JOY!

FOR THE LORD TAKES DELIGHT IN HIS PEOPLE;HE
CROWNS THE HUMBLE WITH VICTORY.
PSALM 149:4 NIV

YOUR STATUTES ARE MY HERITAGE FOREVER; THEY ARE
THE JOY OF MY HEART.
PSALM 119:11 NIV

JOY!

NO, DESPITE ALL THESE THINGS, OVERWHELMING
VICTORY IS OURS THROUGH CHRIST, WHO LOVED US.
ROMANS 8:37 NLT

MY HEART AND SOUL EXPLODE WITH JOY—FULL OF GLORY! EVEN MY BODY WILL REST CONFIDENT AND SECURE.
PSALM 16:9 TPT

JOY!

LET ME HEAR THE SOUNDS OF JOY AND GLADNESS; AND
THOUGH YOU HAVE CRUSHED ME AND BROKEN ME, I
WILL BE HAPPY ONCE AGAIN.
PSALM 51:9 GNT

LET US COME BEFORE HIM WITH THANKSGIVING AND
SING JOYFUL SONGS OF PRAISE.
PSALM 95:2 GNT

JOY!

I FIND JOY IN THE WAY [SHOWN BY] YOUR WRITTEN
INSTRUCTIONS MORE THAN I FIND JOY IN ALL KINDS OF
RICHES.
PSALM 119:14A GWT

I HAVE TOLD YOU THIS SO THAT MY JOY MAY BE IN YOU
AND THAT YOUR JOY MAY BE COMPLETE.
JOHN 15:11 NIV

JOY!

I WILL BE FILLED WITH JOY BECAUSE OF YOU. I WILL
SING PRAISES TO YOUR NAME, O MOST HIGH.
PSALM 9:2 NLT

EVEN THOUGH YOU DON'T SEE HIM NOW, YOU TRUST HIM
AND SO REJOICE WITH A GLORIOUS JOY THAT IS TOO
MUCH FOR WORDS.
1 PETER 1:8B CEB

JOY!

MANY SORROWS COME TO THE WICKED, BUT UNFAILING
LOVE SURROUNDS THOSE WHO TRUST THE LORD
PSALM 32:10 NLT

JOY!

TRUST IN THE LORD FOREVER, FOR THE LORD,
THE LORD HIMSELF, IS THE ROCK ETERNAL.
ISAIAH 26:4 NIV

BUT I TRUST YOUR MERCY. MY HEART FINDS JOY IN YOUR
SALVATION.
PSALM 13:5 GW

BUT THE ANGEL SAID TO THEM, "DO NOT BE AFRAID. I
BRING YOU GOOD NEWS THAT WILL CAUSE GREAT JOY
FOR ALL THE PEOPLE."
LUKE 2:10 NIV

JOY!

CLAP YOUR HANDS, ALL YOU PEOPLES! SHOUT TO GOD
WITH A LOUD CRY OF JOY!
PSALM 47:1 ISV

_____

_____

_____

_____

_____

_____

_____

_____

_____

_____

_____

_____

_____

_____

_____

_____

_____

_____

_____

_____

YOU HAVE ENLARGED THE NATION AND INCREASED THEIR
JOY; THEY REJOICE BEFORE YOU AS PEOPLE REJOICE AT
THE HARVEST
ISAIAH 9:3 NIV

SHOUT ALOUD AND SING FOR JOY, PEOPLE OF ZION,
FOR GREAT IS THE HOLY ONE OF ISRAEL AMONG YOU.
ISAIAH 12:6 NIV

_____

_____

_____

_____

_____

_____

_____

_____

_____

_____

_____

_____

_____

_____

_____

_____

_____

_____

_____

_____

_____

BUT I AM LIKE AN OLIVE TREE, THRIVING IN THE HOUSE
OF GOD. I WILL ALWAYS TRUST IN GOD'S UNFAILING
LOVE.
PSALM 52:8 NLT

JOY!

DON'T BE PULLED IN DIFFERENT DIRECTIONS OR
WORRIED ABOUT A THING. BE SATURATED IN
PRAYER...OFFERING YOUR FAITH-FILLED REQUESTS
BEFORE GOD WITH OVERFLOWING GRATITUDE...
PHILIPPIANS 4:6 TPT

AS WE TRUST, WE REJOICE WITH AN UNCONTAINED JOY
FLOWING FROM YAHWEH!
PSALM 33:21 TPT

JOY!

THE LORD PROTECTS AND DEFENDS ME; I TRUST IN HIM.
HE GIVES ME HELP AND MAKES ME GLAD; I PRAISE HIM
WITH JOYFUL SONGS.
PSALM 28:7 GNT

I WILL INSTRUCT YOU AND TEACH YOU IN THE WAY YOU
SHOULD GO; I WILL COUNSEL YOU WITH MY LOVING
EYE ON YOU.
PSALM 32:8 NIV

JOY!

SO GOD BROUGHT OUT HIS CHOSEN ONES WITH
SINGING; WITH A JOYFUL SHOUT THEY WERE SET FREE!
PSALM 105:43 TPT

JOY!

AND FASTEN YOUR THOUGHTS ON EVERY GLORIOUS
WORK OF GOD, PRAISING HIM ALWAYS.
PHILIPPIANS 4:8B TPT

JOY!

CONSIDER IT PURE JOY, MY BROTHERS AND SISTERS,
WHENEVER YOU FACE TRIALS OF MANY KINDS.
JAMES 1:2 NIV

JOY!

MY SOUL WILL FIND JOY IN THE LORD AND BE JOYFUL
ABOUT HIS SALVATION.
PSALM 35:9 GW

JOY!

HONOR AND MAJESTY SURROUND HIM; STRENGTH AND
JOY FILL HIS DWELLING.
1 CHRONICLES 16:27 NLT

BUT LET ALL WHO TAKE REFUGE IN YOU REJOICE; LET
THEM SING JOYFUL PRAISES FOREVER.
PSALM 5:11A NLT

JOY!

THEY TOLD THEM—MUCH TO EVERYONE'S JOY—THAT THE
GENTILES, TOO, WERE BEING CONVERTED.
ACTS 15:3A NLT

SO REJOICE IN THE LORD AND BE GLAD, ALL YOU WHO
OBEY HIM! SHOUT FOR JOY, ALL YOU WHOSE HEARTS
ARE PURE!
PSALM 32:11 NLT

THEY WILL ENTER ZION WITH SINGING; EVERLASTING
JOY WILL CROWN THEIR HEADS. GLADNESS AND JOY
WILL OVERTAKE THEM, AND SORROW...WILL FLEE AWAY.
ISAIAH 35:10 NIV

_____

_____

_____

_____

_____

_____

_____

_____

_____

_____

_____

_____

_____

_____

_____

_____

_____

_____

_____

_____

TASTE AND SEE THAT THE LORD IS GOOD. OH, THE JOYS
OF THOSE WHO TAKE REFUGE IN HIM!
PSALM 34:8 NLT

LET THE TREES OF THE FOREST SING FOR JOY BEFORE
THE LORD...GIVE THANKS TO THE LORD, FOR HE IS
GOOD!
1 CHRONICLES 16:33-34 NLT

JOY!

I HAVE TOLD YOU THESE THINGS, SO THAT IN ME YOU
MAY HAVE PEACE.
JOHN 16:33 NIV

JOY!

THE LORD GIVES STRENGTH TO HIS PEOPLE;
THE LORD BLESSES HIS PEOPLE WITH PEACE.
PSALM 29:11 NIV

PRAISE GOD WITH SHOUTS OF JOY, ALL PEOPLE!
PSALM 66:1 GNT

FOR THE KINGDOM OF GOD IS NOT A MATTER OF
EATING AND DRINKING, BUT OF RIGHTEOUSNESS, PEACE
AND JOY IN THE HOLY SPIRIT,
ROMANS 14:17 NIV

IN HIM OUR HEARTS FIND JOY. IN HIS HOLY NAME WE
TRUST.
PSALM 33:21 GW

JOY!

WITH JOY YOU WILL DRINK DEEPLY FROM THE FOUNTAIN
OF SALVATION... TELL THE NATIONS WHAT HE HAS
DONE...
ISAIAH 12:3-4 NLT

JOY!

EVEN THE WILDERNESS AND DESERT WILL BE GLAD IN
THOSE DAYS. THE WASTELAND WILL REJOICE ....
ISAIAH 35:1 NIV

JOY!

SHOUT WITH JOY TO THE LORD, ALL THE EARTH!
PSALM 100:1 NLT

_____

_____

_____

_____

_____

_____

_____

_____

_____

_____

_____

_____

_____

_____

_____

_____

_____

_____

_____

_____

_____

THE LORD SAID, "SING FOR JOY, PEOPLE OF
JERUSALEM! I AM COMING TO LIVE AMONG YOU!"
ZECHARIAH 2:10 GNT

JOY!

RIGHTEOUS PEOPLE WILL FIND JOY IN THE LORD AND
TAKE REFUGE IN HIM.
PSALM 64:10A GW

SING AND SHOUT FOR JOY, PEOPLE OF ISRAEL! REJOICE
WITH ALL YOUR HEART, JERUSALEM!
ZEPHANIAH 3:14 GNT

JOY!

REJOICE GREATLY, DAUGHTER ZION! ...SEE, YOUR KING
COMES TO YOU, RIGHTEOUS AND HAVING SALVATION,
ZECHARIAH 9:9A NIV

JOY!

GOD OUR SAVIOR SHOWED US HOW GOOD AND KIND
HE IS.
TITUS 3:4 CEV

JOY!

YOUR KINDNESS WILL REWARD YOU, BUT YOUR CRUELTY
WILL DESTROY YOU.
PROVERBS 11:17 NLT

BE KIND AND COMPASSIONATE TO ONE ANOTHER,
FORGIVING EACH OTHER, JUST AS IN CHRIST GOD
FORGAVE YOU.
EPHESIANS 4:32 NIV

JOY!

YOU ARE THE PEOPLE OF GOD; HE LOVED YOU AND
CHOSE YOU FOR HIS OWN. SO THEN, YOU MUST
CLOTHE YOURSELVES WITH COMPASSION, KINDNESS,
HUMILITY, GENTLENESS, AND PATIENCE.
COLOSSIANS 3:12 GNT

YOUR BLESSINGS ARE WITH HIM FOREVER, AND YOUR
PRESENCE FILLS HIM WITH JOY.
PSALM 21:6 GNT

BUT REJOICE INASMUCH AS YOU PARTICIPATE IN THE
SUFFERINGS OF CHRIST, SO THAT YOU MAY BE
OVERJOYED WHEN HIS GLORY IS REVEALED.
1 PETER 4:13 NIV

BE KIND AND HONEST AND YOU WILL LIVE A LONG LIFE;
OTHERS WILL RESPECT YOU AND TREAT YOU FAIRLY.
PROVERBS 21:21 GNT

JOY!

THEY WILL COME AND SHOUT FOR JOY ON THE HEIGHTS
OF ZION; THEY WILL REJOICE IN THE BOUNTY OF THE
LORD...
JEREMIAH 31:12A NIV

JOY!

EVEN THE WILDERNESS AND DESERT WILL BE GLAD IN
THOSE DAYS. THE WASTELAND WILL REJOICE ....
ISAIAH 35:1 NIV

I WILL TURN THEIR MOURNING INTO JOY. I WILL
...EXCHANGE THEIR SORROW FOR REJOICING.
JEREMIAH 31:13B NLT

JOY!

REJOICE AND BE GLAD, BECAUSE GREAT IS YOUR
REWARD IN HEAVEN.
MATTHEW 5:12A NIV

_____

_____

_____

_____

_____

_____

_____

_____

_____

_____

_____

_____

_____

_____

_____

_____

_____

_____

_____

_____

_____

_____

...I CAN CONTINUE TO HELP ALL OF YOU GROW AND
EXPERIENCE THE JOY OF YOUR FAITH.
PHILLIPIANS 1:25B NLT

AT HIS SACRED TENT I WILL SACRIFICE WITH SHOUTS OF
JOY; I WILL SING AND MAKE MUSIC TO THE LORD.
PSALM 27:6 NIV

JOY!

THEY WILL RAVE IN CELEBRATION OF YOUR ABUNDANT
GOODNESS;THEY WILL SHOUT JOYFULLY ABOUT YOUR
RIGHTEOUSNESS
PSALM 145:7 CEB

GIVE THANKS TO THE LORD, FOR HE IS GOOD! HIS
FAITHFUL LOVE ENDURES FOREVER.
PSALM 107:1 NLT

JOY!

... AND YOU WILL REJOICE IN ALL YOU HAVE
ACCOMPLISHED BECAUSE THE LORD YOUR GOD HAS
BLESSED YOU.
DEUTERONOMY 12:7B NLT

LET THEM BRING SONGS OF THANKSGIVING AS THEIR
SACRIFICE. LET THEM TELL IN JOYFUL SONGS WHAT HE
HAS DONE.
PSALM 107:22 GW

SONGS OF JOY AND VICTORY ARE SUNG IN THE CAMP
OF THE GODLY. THE STRONG RIGHT ARM OF THE LORD
HAS DONE GLORIOUS THINGS!
PSALM 118:15 NLT

EVERYONE HAS HEARD ABOUT YOUR OBEDIENCE, SO I
REJOICE BECAUSE OF YOU;
ROMANS 16:19A NIV

JOY!

THE PEOPLE OF EPHRAIM WILL BECOME LIKE MIGHTY
SOLDIERS... THEIR HEARTS WILL FIND JOY IN THE LORD
ZECHARIAH 10:7 ISV

SING AND SHOUT FOR JOY, PEOPLE OF ISRAEL! REJOICE
WITH ALL YOUR HEART, JERUSALEM!
ZEPHANIAH 3:14 GNT

JOY!

MAY YOUR PRIESTS BE CLOTHED IN GODLINESS; MAY
YOUR LOYAL SERVANTS SING FOR JOY.
PSALM 132:9 NLT

JOY!

SHOUT FOR JOY TO THE LORD, ALL THE EARTH, BURST
INTO JUBILANT SONG WITH MUSIC
PSALM 98:4 NIV

JOY!

HE SETS THE TIME FOR SORROW AND THE TIME FOR
JOY, THE TIME FOR MOURNING AND THE TIME FOR
DANCING,
ECCLESIASTES 3:4 GNT

ON THE SEVENTH DAY GOD HAD FINISHED HIS WORK OF
CREATION, SO HE RESTED FROM ALL HIS WORK.
GENESIS 2:2 NLT

BUT MAY THE RIGHTEOUS BE GLAD AND REJOICE
BEFORE GOD; MAY THEY BE HAPPY AND JOYFUL.
PSALM 68:3 NIV

JOY!

HE WILL ONCE AGAIN FILL YOUR MOUTH WITH LAUGHTER
AND YOUR LIPS WITH SHOUTS OF JOY.
JOB 8:21 NLT

FIND JOY IN THE LORD, YOU RIGHTEOUS PEOPLE. GIVE
THANKS TO HIM AS YOU REMEMBER HOW HOLY HE IS.
PSALM 97:12 GW

...BE JOYFUL. GROW TO MATURITY. ENCOURAGE EACH
OTHER. LIVE IN HARMONY AND PEACE....
2 CORINTHIANS 13:11 NLT

JOY!

...I REJOICE, AND I SHARE MY JOY WITH ALL OF YOU.
PHILIPPIANS 2:17 ISV

WE ALSO PRAY THAT YOU WILL BE STRENGTHENED WITH
ALL HIS GLORIOUS POWER...MAY YOU BE FILLED WITH JOY
COLOSSIANS 1:11 NLT

BE JOYFUL IN HOPE, PATIENT IN AFFLICTION, FAITHFUL
IN PRAYER.
ROMANS 12:12 NIV

_____

_____

_____

_____

_____

_____

_____

_____

_____

_____

_____

_____

_____

_____

_____

_____

_____

_____

_____

_____

_____

_____

_____

_____

HOW CAN WE THANK GOD ENOUGH FOR YOU IN RETURN
FOR ALL THE JOY WE HAVE IN THE PRESENCE OF OUR
GOD BECAUSE OF YOU?
1 THESSALONIANS 3:9 NIV

JOY!

YOUR LOVE HAS GIVEN ME GREAT JOY AND
ENCOURAGEMENT, BECAUSE YOU, BROTHER, HAVE
REFRESHED THE HEARTS OF THE LORD'S PEOPLE.
PHILEMON 1:7 NIV

JOY!

THIS IS OUR GOD! WE'VE WAITED FOR HIM, AND HE
SAVED US! ...WE WILL KEEP SHOUTING WITH JOY AS WE
FIND OUR BLISS IN HIS SALVATION...
ISAIAH 25:9 TPT

JOY!

YOU HAVE GIVEN THEM GREAT JOY, LORD; YOU HAVE
MADE THEM HAPPY. THEY REJOICE..AS PEOPLE
REJOICE WHEN THEY HARVEST GRAIN....
ISAIAH 9:3 GNT

JOY!

YES, YOU SHOULD REJOICE, AND I WILL SHARE YOUR
JOY.
PHILIPPIANS 2:18 NLT

ALWAYS BE FULL OF JOY IN THE LORD. I SAY IT AGAIN—
REJOICE!
PHILIPPIANS 4:4 NLT

JOY!

...REJOICE IN THE LORD YOUR GOD! FOR THE RAIN HE
SENDS DEMONSTRATES HIS FAITHFULNESS.
JOEL 2:23 NLT

JOY!

WE ASK HIM TO STRENGTHEN YOU BY HIS GLORIOUS
MIGHT WITH ALL THE POWER YOU NEED TO PATIENTLY
ENDURE EVERYTHING WITH JOY.
COLOSSIANS 1:11 GW

JOY!

MAY ALL WHO ARE GODLY REJOICE IN THE LORD AND
PRAISE HIS HOLY NAME!
PSALM 97:12 NLT

JOY!

GLORY IN HIS HOLY NAME; LET THE HEARTS OF THOSE
WHO SEEK THE LORD REJOICE.
PSALM 105:3 NIV

JOY!

YET I WILL REJOICE IN THE LORD, I WILL BE JOYFUL IN
GOD MY SAVIOR.
HABAKKUK 3:18 NIV

JOY!

ALWAYS BE JOYFUL.
1 THESSALONIANS 5:16S 5:16 NLT